THEO WALCOTT

FOOTBALL ALL-STARS

RORY CALLAN

Theo Walcott is one of England's most exciting players – he moves like lightning! Read all about his club and international football career inside – then flip over to find out more about Steven Gerrard.

EDGE
W
FRANKLIN
WATTS

LONDON·SYDNEY

First published in 2012 by
Franklin Watts
338 Euston Road
London NW1 3BH

Franklin Watts Australia
Level 17/207 Kent Street
Sydney NSW 2000

Series editor: Adrian Cole
Art director: Jonathan Hair
Design: Steve Prosser
Picture research: Diana Morris

A CIP catalogue record of this book
is available from the British Library

ISBN: 978 1 4451 0211 5

Dewey classification: 796.3'34'092

Printed in China

Franklin Watts is a division of
Hachette Children's Books,
an Hachette UK company.
www.hachette.co.uk

Theo Walcott
Contents

Hat-trick Hero

**Croatia vs England – 10 September, 2008.
Stadion Maksimir, Zagreb, Croatia.**

8:45 pm

The England team are in Croatia for a crucial World Cup
Group 6 qualifying match. This will be a tough game –
Croatia have never lost an international match at home.
Theo Walcott, the youngest person ever to play for England,
is replacing David Beckham on the right wing. The pressure
is on – Walcott has got to show his new boss, Fabio Capello,
that he has what it takes to be an England player.

9.25 pm

With 25 minutes of the first half gone, two of Croatia's defenders fail to clear the ball. It rebounds to Walcott on the edge of the **penalty box**. He runs forward and from a narrow angle squeezes the ball into the far corner of the net. GOAL! The few England fans in the stadium celebrate wildly. Walcott is bursting with pride – he has just scored his first goal for England!

10:13 pm (13 minutes in to the second half)

Walcott's pace is terrifying Croatia's defenders. A cross from Wayne Rooney lands at Walcott's feet. In an almost identical goal to the first one, Walcott manages to arrow the ball past the goalkeeper. GOAL! England are 2–0 up!

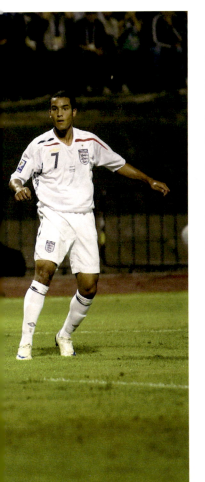

10:36 (81 minutes in to the game)

With only 9 minutes to go England are leading 3–1, but Walcott isn't finished yet. Another perfect ball from Rooney splits Croatia's defence, setting Walcott up for a one-on-one with the goalkeeper. He side foots the ball past the keeper and runs off to salute the England fans. GOAL! The Croatia fans fall silent. Walcott has just created football history by becoming the youngest player to score a **hat trick** for England. ***But how did he get there?***

◄ *Theo Walcott watches his shot fly past Croatia's goalkeeper to put England 1–0 up.*

v

RAW TALENT

Theodore James Walcott was born on 16 March, 1989 in London, but he was brought up in Compton in Newbury. He had no interest in football as a young boy, and went to his first football skills class when he was ten years old. The coach noticed that Walcott was incredibly fast and skilful with the ball. He rang Theo's father and said: "I think Theo has got something special."

AFC Newbury

Within a few days Walcott's dad took him along to the local football club, AFC Newbury. After Walcott's first football match there he had scored a hat trick. Nobody there on the day could have imagined that in just seven years, Walcott would be playing for England.

Swindon and Southampton

Walcott was determined not to let his talent go to waste. He practised in the morning, during lunchtime, after school and even in the house after it got dark.

▲ *Walcott, aged 8, in his Compton Primary School uniform.*

▲ *Walcott (circled) with his AFC Newbury team-mates in about 1999.*

Walcott went on to score 100 goals for AFC Newbury in his first season. This attracted the attention of **team scouts**. In 2000, he **signed for** Swindon's youth team. Then he took up a scholarship at Southampton FC, who were in the Premier League. At school, Walcott became the best player in the district. In one game he had to be **substituted** because the opposition players kept trying to injure him. He had scored 9 goals – with 20 minutes left to play!

Premier League debut

Walcott continued to amaze the Southampton staff. The 14-year-old could control the ball well, and run 100 metres in 11.5 seconds. In 2004, he made his **debut** for the Southampton first team, scoring the winning goal against Leeds United.

TOP GUN

Walcott's performances at Southampton were attracting attention from the country's top Premier League managers. They could clearly see that Walcott was a future England international. He had scored 5 goals in 11 games playing with the England Under-17s. Liverpool, Chelsea and Arsenal all put in an offer for him.

▼ *Walcott takes on two defenders during a match for Southampton.*

Arsenal FC

Although he was a Liverpool supporter, he felt the club was too far away from his family and friends. Chelsea offered a huge amount of money, but Walcott wanted to move to Arsenal. He knew that when it came to developing young, talented players, Arsene Wenger was one of the best managers in the world. Another important reason was that Thierry Henry, Walcott's favourite player, was the star player for Arsenal at the time. He was sure that under the guidance of Wenger and Henry, his career would progress at Arsenal.

Walcott signed for Arsenal in January 2006 for £12 million, the highest amount ever paid for a 16-year-old. His life was now set to change forever. Southampton had been paying him £90 a week; now he could expect to make millions.

At Arsenal, Walcott began to learn about life at one of the biggest and most successful clubs in the world. After his first training session, he knew he was going to improve his game. The speed and movement of the Arsenal players was in a different league to what he was used to at Southampton.

▲ *Walcott slots through a pass for Arsenal against Hamburg SV in 2006.*

Arsenal Teen Debut

Walcott now set his sights on securing a place on the Arsenal first team. His debut against Aston Villa on the opening day of the 2006/07 season was an historic day for Walcott and for Arsenal FC. For the previous 120 years, Arsenal had played all their home games at Highbury. Now, for the first time, the team was playing at its new stadium, the Emirates.

The Emirates Stadium

On a beautiful August day in North London, the Emirates was packed with 60,000 supporters. With just 17 minutes to go, Walcott came on as a substitute. The Arsenal fans applauded loudly. They had heard and read so much about this wonder kid – now they were going to get a chance to see what he was made of.

Walcott didn't disappoint. His pace down the wing was a constant danger to the Aston Villa defence, and he capped off a fine display by setting up Arsenal's equalising goal. It was the beginning of a new era for the club. Walcott felt honoured to make his debut on such a day.

▶ *Walcott controls the ball during a match at the Emirates Stadium.*

Arsene Wenger, Arsenal manager

Arsene Wenger is regarded by many as the best **coach** in the world at developing young players. Wenger only played Walcott in every second or third game during the year. Young players can suffer serious injury if they play too many games early in their professional careers. It takes time to adjust to the demands of a full season in top-flight football. Walcott got time to rest between matches and avoid injuries.

By the end of the 2007/2008 season, Walcott was an Arsenal first team regular. He scored goals, but more importantly, created chances for his team with his pace and trickery down the wing. Walcott knew he had made it to the top of the Premier League when Arsene Wenger gave him the number 14 shirt. This had been Thierry Henry's number and it has a special significance for Arsenal fans.

Speed and intelligence

Walcott is without doubt the fastest player in the Premier League. He can now run 100 metres in an

▶ *Walcott pops the ball past the goalkeeper in a Champions League match against Villareal.*

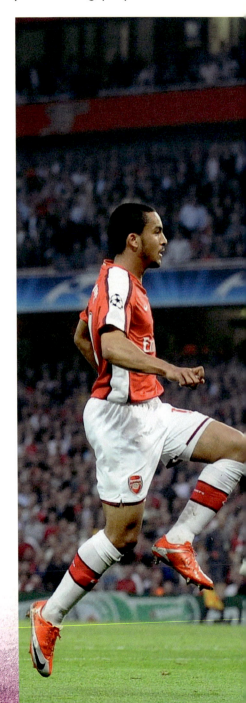

incredibly fast 10.30 seconds. But there is more to Walcott's game than just sheer pace. He seems to know where the ball is going to land – an important quality for a winger to have.

Arsenal vs Barcelona, UEFA Champions League quarter-final, first leg

One of his outstanding displays over the last few seasons was against one of the best teams in the world, Barcelona FC. The match took place at the Emirates Stadium on 31 March, 2010. Barcelona dominated the first half. Then they scored two goals in the first 20 minutes of the second half, making the score 2–0. They continued to batter the Arsenal midfield and defence. Then Walcott came on as a substitute. Within minutes he had turned the game around. He scored Arsenal's first goal and tormented the Barcelona defence with his pace and skill.

▼ *Walcott shoots and scores against Barcelona in 2010.*

▲ *Walcott celebrates with Arsenal team-mate Abou Diaby after scoring.*

Thanks to Walcott's energy and pace, Arsenal now took the game to Barcelona. With five minutes remaining they pressed forward and Cesc Fabregas scored a late **equaliser** to give Arsenal a deserved draw. Argentinian star, Lionel Messi, later described Walcott as:

"one of the most dangerous players I have played against".

With each season Walcott gains more experience and every year his goal-scoring record improves. Arsene Wenger said that he wants Walcott to play as a striker, instead of as a winger. With his pace, Walcott is sure to cause many defenders a lot of sleepless nights.

ENGLAND UNDER-21s

In 2006, and at just 15 years old, Walcott had secured his place on the England Under-17 team. Then in 2007, Walcott helped the England Under-21s reach the semi-final of the European Championships. In 2009 they went one step further by reaching the final for the first time ever.

▼ Walcott shoots and scores for the England U-21s against Moldova in 2006.

International Caps

When Walcott joined the Under-21s in the summer of 2006, he was in the unique position of having already played for the England senior team. Walcott enjoyed the training with the Under-21s. The other teenagers were around his age and the atmosphere was relaxed. There was lots of joking between everyone on the team. It was a big change from the tense pressure of the 2006 World Cup training camp. Some things remained the same for Walcott though – he was still the youngest member of the squad!

Under-21s debut

Walcott made his debut against Moldova in August 2006. Within three minutes he had broken another national record when he scored the opening goal of the game. He become the youngest ever player to score for the Under-21s – at just 17 years old.

Under-21 European Championship Finals 2009

In 2009, the Under-21 European Championship Finals were hosted by Sweden. England had top Premier League players Gabriel Agbonlahor, James Milner, Steven Taylor and Micah Richards in the squad, so the team was feeling confident. Walcott was really excited to be actually playing in his first international tournament.

The Under-21 manager, Stuart Pearce, prepared the young side for the opening game. He told them that this was a once in a lifetime opportunity. The most important thing was that they enjoy it.

Opening games

Pearce's advice seemed to work. England's first game of the tournament against Finland went well. Micah Richards scored with a header late on, making it 2–1 and collecting maximum points. Next up were the pre-tournament favourites, Spain. England recorded a well deserved 2–0 victory. Walcott played his part by setting up the second goal for James Milner, after a blistering run through the Spain defence.

All the way to the final

After winning the opening two games, England were on a roll. They went on to defeat Sweden in the semi-final after a **penalty shootout**. This set up a final meeting with Germany. Unfortunately, England had a lot of injuries and **suspensions** heading into the final. With the team missing all of its strikers due to injury, Walcott had to play up front on his own. Despite a huge effort from every England player available, it just wasn't enough to defeat Germany.

England lost the European final, but the whole experience was valuable for Walcott and his team-mates. They had proven to themselves that they had the ability to get to the final of a major international tournament. With so much high-quality talent coming through the ranks, the future of the England football team looks to be in safe hands.

▶ *Walcott runs away from Germany's Benedikt Höwedes during the U-21s European Championship final in 2009.*

WORLD CUP FINALS

Walcott trained hard and kept his skills sharp. His commitment was repaid when he was selected to make his full England international debut. The friendly match was against Hungary at Old Trafford. When Walcott ran on to the pitch he became the youngest ever England player, at only 17 years and 75 days. Even today it is unusual for someone so young to make it on to a national football team. England beat Hungary 3–1. After the game Walcott's mum and dad met him in the players **VIP** area. They were extremely proud of their son. There was a great buzz of excitement in the air – everyone was talking about travelling to Germany for the 2006 World Cup Finals.

World Cup selection

England qualified comfortably for the 2006 World Cup Finals, finishing top of their group. Soon it was time to announce the 23-man squad that would travel to Germany. Sven-Goran Eriksson, the England manager, surprised everyone by including Walcott. Erikson felt that the teenager had the kind of magic needed to make an impact. But at this time Walcott had yet to make his Arsenal debut.

Walcott gets the news

Walcott's inclusion in the World Cup squad shocked him as much as anyone else. On the day the squad was announced he was taking his driving theory test. When he came out of the exam, he got a call from his dad telling him he'd been selected. Walcott nearly dropped his phone – how could this be possible? He had just started playing for the Arsenal reserve team.

▲ *Walcott powers up a shot during a friendly between England and Hungary.*

ENGLAND YOUNG GUN

The training sessions in Germany were tough. Every player was focused and fighting for a place on the World Cup starting 11. Walcott was nervous at first. He was afraid of making mistakes. It took him a few days, but he eventually beat his nerves. His team-mates were very supportive, especially defenders John Terry and Gary Neville, who advised him on how to handle hard-hitting defenders. By the time England were knocked out of the World Cup Finals, Walcott was performing brilliantly in training. Walcott hadn't been picked to play, but that didn't stop him supporting his teammates.

World Cup Finals 2010

Walcott didn't make the selection for the 2010 World Cup Finals held in South Africa. His exclusion by Fabio Capello, the England manager, was another surprise. Capello later said:

"[Walcott] is one of the players after the World Cup I thought about a lot. I made a mistake not selecting him."

European Championships 2012

Walcott soon got over the disappointment of missing the World Cup. Now he set his sights on helping England to qualify for Euro 2012 in Poland and

▶ *Walcott scores for England during their World Cup qualifying match against Croatia in Group 6, 2008.*

Ukraine. He created some crucial goals for England during the qualifying campaign, and helped them to the top of Group G.

In November 2011, Walcott was on the England team that beat Spain – the current World Champions. Walcott has become part of one of the most attacking and exciting England teams in years.

Timeline Glossary

Team	Appearances	Goals
League		
2004–2006 Southampton	21	4
2006– Arsenal	125	20
National		
2004–2005 England U-16	4	0
2005–2006 England U-17	14	0
2006 England U-19	1	0
2006–2010 England U-21	20	6
2006– England	20	3

Coach Someone who trains athletes.

Debut First appearance, in this case as a player in a particular team.

Equaliser Used to describe the goal that brings both teams to the same score.

Hat trick Three goals scored by one player in one match.

Penalty box A marked rectangle on a football pitch, with the goal in the centre, inside which players take penalty shots.

Penalty shootout In the event of a draw, players from each team take it in turns to score goals from the penalty spot.

Quarter-final Eight teams compete in the quarter-finals in order to win a place in the semi-finals.

Signed (for) Signed a contract that committed the player to a football club.

Substituted Replaced with another player.

Suspension If a player is sent off for foul play, he will then have to miss the next match or so before he is allowed to play again for his team.

Team scouts Football coaches on the look out for talented young players to join their team.

VIP Very Important Person.

Index

STEVEN GERRARD

FOOTBALL ALL-STARS

RORY CALLAN

Steven Gerrard
is one of the
most consistent
footballers in the
world. Read all
about his club
and international
football career
inside – then flip
over to find
out more about
Theo Walcott.

EDGE
FRANKLIN WATTS

LONDON·SYDNEY

First published in 2012 by
Franklin Watts
338 Euston Road
London NW1 3BH

Franklin Watts Australia
Level 17/207 Kent Street
Sydney NSW 2000

Series editor: Adrian Cole
Art director: Jonathan Hair
Design: Steve Prosser
Picture research: Diana Morris

A CIP catalogue record of this book
is available from the British Library

ISBN: 978 1 4451 0211 5

Dewey classification: 796.3'34'092

Printed in China

Franklin Watts is a division of
Hachette Children's Books,
an Hachette UK company.
www.hachette.co.uk

Acknowledgements:
AFP/Getty Images: XIX. Back Page
Images/Rex Features: XV. Roy
Beardsworth/Rex Features: XVI. Peter
Bennet/Rex Features: 14. Shaun Botterill/
FIFA/Getty Images: 23. Graham
Chadwick/Daily Mail/Rex Features: XI,
XII-XIII. Phil Cole/Getty Images: XXIII. Adrian
Dennis/AFP/Getty Images: XIV. Empics/
Topfoto: 8-9. Mitchell Gunn/Action
Plus: Walcott cover. Tim Hales/AP/PAI:
Gerrard cover. Martin Hayhow/AFP/Getty
Images: VIII. Andy Hooper/Daily Mail/Rex
Features: 5, 11, 13, 17, IV-V, XXI. Mike
Leech/Rex Features: IX. Liverpool Post &
Echo: 7. Rebecca Naden/PA/Topfoto: 15.
PA/Topfoto: 12. Geoff Pugh/Rex Features:
18-19. Rex Features: VI, VII. Clive Rose/
Getty Images: 21.

Note: At the time of going to press, the
statistics in this book were up to date.
However, due to the nature of sport, it is
possible that some of these may now be
out of date.

STEVEN GERRARD
CONTENTS

The Making of a Lionheart

**World Cup 2002 qualifier, Germany vs England –
1 September, 2001, Munich, Germany.**

6:45 pm

It's 45 minutes before kickoff. 21-year-old **midfielder** Steven
Gerrard and his England team-mates take their seats in the away
dressing room. The players know that England have never beaten
Germany on German soil, and Gerrard is feeling nervous. This is
only his sixth time in the national team, and it is by far his biggest
test so far. He receives the number 4 shirt from the kit man. One
question keeps turning over in his mind, "Am I ready for this?"

7:15 pm, 15 minutes to kick off

The England dressing room is buzzing. After a few words from the
England manager, Sven-Goran Eriksson, and team captain, David
Beckham, Gerrard is feeling a lot more confident. There is a huge
roar from the England players before they burst out of the dressing
room door. They line up beside the Germany team, and begin
their march onto the pitch.

7:36 pm

GOAL! Germany score after only 5 minutes – it's not looking
good for England. But in the 12th minute Michael Owen scores
an equaliser for England.

8:17 pm

It's two minutes into injury time at the end of the first half, when a cross finds Rio Ferdinand, who heads the ball down to Gerrard. He controls the ball with his chest then smashes a low shot past the Germany goalkeeper from 30 yards out. It is a sensational goal that puts England into a 2–1 lead!

9:20 pm

At the end of the match the referee blows the final whistle. The England players and fans start celebrating. The scoreboard reads Germany 1 – England 5! Gerrard is jumping up and down in

delight. He has just played in an incredible match, with England having scored another three goals in the second half. Gerrard put in a fantastic performance and proved that he was ready for the big games.

But how did he get there?

▲ *Gerrard fires an unstoppable shot past the Germany goalkeeper to make the score 2–1.*

STARTING OUT

Steven Gerrard was born in Liverpool on 30 May, 1980. He grew up on the tough housing estate of Huyton in the east of the city. He lived with his mum, dad and older brother, Paul. His dad was a lifelong Liverpool fan. He took Steven and his brother to matches at Anfield.

As a kid, Gerrard was obsessed with Liverpool and with football. He learned his skills on the streets of Huyton, playing football with kids from all over the estate. To survive in these games you had to be tough. A lot of the boys he played against were two or three years older than him, but Gerrard made sure he didn't get pushed around. It was a good training ground for him and taught him how to be strong.

Serious accident

Life could have turned out very differently for Gerrard. When he was nine he was involved in an accident which could have killed his football career. While playing football on waste ground near his home, he went to kick a ball out of a patch of nettles. Instead of kicking the ball, he hit an old garden fork which went straight through his foot. Gerrard was rushed to hospital. The doctors feared that they would have to amputate (cut off) his foot. Luckily, a skilful surgeon was able to treat the wound and it eventually healed. The surgeon saved Gerrard's foot, and also saved his future football career.

▲ *Steven Gerrard (holding the ball) in his 1990 football team.*

LEARNING HIS TRADE

When Gerrard was 8 years old, he started training at Liverpool's Centre for Excellence. Here, talented young footballers from all over Liverpool were given top-class coaching. On his first day he met Michael Owen, who was set to become another future England star. When Gerrard turned 15, Liverpool offered him a two-year **apprentice contract** with a wage of £50 a week. His dream had come true – he was playing football for the club he loved.

Liverpool first team debut

Gerrard made his **debut** for the Liverpool first team at Anfield against Blackburn Rovers in November 1998. He came on as a substitute with two minutes to go. It was a proud day for Steven and his family. After all the years of hard work and dedication he was finally able to run out onto the Anfield turf. To hear his name announced over the speakers in the stadium and hear the cheers from the Kop must have been like a dream come true for him.

▶ *Liverpool fans hold up their scarves on the Kop at Anfield in 1994.*

ROAD TO GLORY

In the 2000/01 season Liverpool won the treble: the League Cup, FA Cup and UEFA Cup, and Gerrard was voted the PFA Young Player of the Year. He also signed a new four-year contract that would earn him £50,000 a week. He was still only 21 years old. Two years later, Gerrard received the biggest honour of all when he was made club captain.

Champions League, 2004/05

In the summer of 2004, Liverpool played a UEFA Champions League qualifying game against AK Graz of Austria. Gerrard scored the only two goals of the match. The 2–0 victory was the start of a long and exciting journey for the Liverpool team. Eight months later they would be playing in the final.

Liverpool vs AC Milan, Champions League Final

The Champions League Final is the biggest club game in the world. On this occasion it was held in Istanbul, the capital of Turkey. When Gerrard led his Liverpool team onto the pitch, he could not hear his team-mates speaking because the noise from the crowd was so loud. Liverpool had a terrible first half. They were outplayed by a very skilful AC Milan team. After 45 minutes, Liverpool were 3–0 down and the match looked over.

At half time the Liverpool players were shattered. Gerrard told the players that if they could get the first goal they would have a chance. In a crisis situation like this, players look to their captain to lead them. By his actions that night, Gerrard proved himself to be a real leader.

▲ *Gerrard leads by example, and attacks the AC Milan defence.*

The second half started, and after just 9 minutes Gerrard scored with a header. GOAL! It was the lifeline Liverpool needed. Then, two minutes later – GOAL – Vladimir Smicer scored Liverpool's second with a long range effort. Liverpool were on a roll! The players could sense that AC Milan were panicking, and they surged forward in search of another goal. Gerrard sprinted into the AC Milan box with one of his trademark forward runs. Just as he was about to shoot, he was flattened by the AC Milan midfielder, Gennaro Gattuso. Penalty! GOAL! Liverpool scored the spot kick and levelled the match at 3–3.

▲ *Gerrard heads the ball towards the AC Milan goal to score Liverpool's first goal of the night.*

Extra time and penalties

After full time, the match was drawn at 3–3. It was still drawn after extra time, so the result would come down to a **penalty shootout**. In the penalty shootout, Andriy Shevchenko of AC Milan had to score their fourth penalty to stay in the match. He fired the ball with a great strike, but his shot was saved by Liverpool's goalkeeper, Jerzy Dudek. Unbelievably, Liverpool were champions of Europe! They had just staged the most dramatic comeback in Champions League Final history.

Gerrard then stepped up on the podium and lifted the Champions League trophy over his head. At 25, he was the second youngest player to captain a team to European glory.

▼ Gerrard celebrates winning the Champions League with his Liverpool team-mates.

ENGLAND DEBUT

Gerrard's England career started badly. When he was 14, he went for trials for the England Under-15 team, but the England coaching staff thought he was too small to play international football. Gerrard was disappointed, but he kept training and practising hard at Liverpool.

The hard work paid off, because he was picked to play for England at Under-16 level. He even went on to captain the Under-18 England team.

◀ *Gerrard lines up in the England first team in 2000.*

England first team

In May 2000, Gerrard's boyhood dream of playing for his country came true when he was picked to start with the England first team. He started in midfield against Ukraine at Wembley Stadium, London. It was an amazing experience for him. With 85,000 in the stadium and millions watching on TV, he knew he had reached the top of the game. England won 2–0, and Gerrard performed well. The England fans were left in no doubt that he was good enough to be a top-class international player.

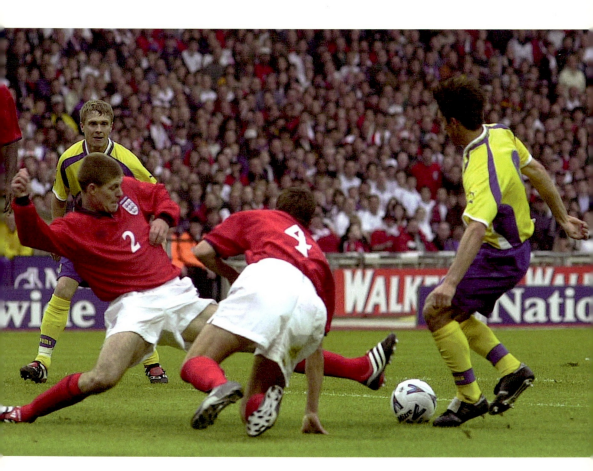

▲ *Gerrard puts pressure on Ukraine in his first game for England.*

South Africa – World Cup 2010

Gerrard enjoyed international football with England for almost a decade. By the time of the World Cup in South Africa 2010, he was the most experienced player in the England squad – with 80 international **caps**. In the 2006 World Cup in Germany, he had been a key member of the team who were eventually knocked out in the **quarter-finals** on penalties. This time around Gerrard was confident that England had enough talented players to make it all the way to the World Cup Final.

In England's private training complex, Gerrard was looking forward to a quiet build-up to the tournament. This all changed after England's very first training session. The England captain, Rio Ferdinand, damaged **ligaments** in his knee that put him out of action. England had lost one of the best defenders, and they needed a new captain.

There was one obvious choice for Fabio Capello, England's manager: Steven Gerrard. As one of the country's greatest ever midfielders, he was certain to start every game for England. He also captained Liverpool, and would be able to cope with the pressure of being England captain.

▲ *Gerrard in training with the England World Cup 2010 squad in Royal Bafokeng Stadium, South Africa.*

England vs USA, World Cup Group C match

The 12 June, 2010, was one of the proudest moments in Gerrard's life. He became only the tenth man to captain the England team at the World Cup Finals. Their opponents were the

USA – a solid team that were ready to give England a tough game. With 30,000 England supporters in the stadium, Gerrard's World Cup couldn't have got off to a better start. He scored after only four minutes! GOAL!

Having made such a positive start to the game, England should have pushed on to win the match. It didn't work out that way. A weak shot from the USA's Clint Dempsey rolled into the net after England's goalkeeper, Rob Green, let the ball roll through his fingers. GOAL! The match finished 1–1.

A 1–1 draw was a disappointing result but not the end of the world. England still had two "easy" games left in Group C. However, they performed poorly against Algeria in the second group game. Then they only narrowly won against Slovenia. England finished second in the group behind the USA. This was bad news. Now England faced their greatest World Cup rivals in the first knockout round: Germany.

◀ *Gerrard races to close down the USA's Landon Donovan during World Cup 2010.*

Germany vs England, World Cup Finals, last 16.

The game took place in the impressive Free State Stadium in Bloemfontein, South Africa. Germany started off brightly, and created some clear goal-scoring chances. England on the other hand did not seem up to the pace of the game. Germany's dominance was rewarded after 19 minutes, when Miroslav Klose got the opening goal. England's defence had been sliced open by a long ball. After another 12 minutes, the same thing happened again when Lukas Podolski scored Germany's second goal. At 2–0 things were looking bad for England.

However, the England players did not give up. In fact, the second goal seemed to wake them up. For the last 15 minutes of the first half England completely dominated the game. On 36 minutes, Matthew Upson scored with a header from a pinpoint cross from Gerrard to make it 2–1. Then, one minute later, a **controversial decision** by the referee rocked the England team.

Goal disallowed

Frank Lampard shot on goal from outside the penalty box. The ball hit the crossbar and bounced into the net, behind the line. Everybody in the stadium and watching on TV at home could see it was a goal. However, the referee ruled that the ball did not cross the line and the goal was not given. The England players were furious. Instead of being level with Germany at half time, England were 2–1 down. England would now have to chase the game against one of the best teams in the world.

▲ *Gerrard stretches to take the ball away from Germany's Per Mertesacker.*

Worst defeat ever

The second half was tough on England. They had to attack and push players forward in order to get an equaliser. This meant that there were gaps left in the England defence. Germany made the most of the situation, and went on to score two more goals from two expertly worked **counterattacks**. England ended up losing 4–1, their worst defeat at the World Cup.

After the game Gerrard was shocked. He couldn't believe that England were going home from the World Cup. He had been one of England's better players, but overall England just couldn't cope with the pace, passing and accuracy of the Germany team.

Gerrard had to face the media to explain why England had failed to perform. As usual, he was honest and to the point. He simply said that England were not good enough, admitting that losing 4–1 to arch-rivals Germany was ***"as low as it gets"***.

England march on

After a long, hard and disappointing World Cup campaign, Gerrard took a well-deserved holiday before the 2010/11 season began. He returned to international duty in September to play in England's 3–0 victory over Bulgaria at Wembley Stadium. It was England's first qualifying game for the 2012 European Championships in Poland and Ukraine. With Gerrard controlling the midfield, England completely dominated the game. And as England look to the future, Gerrard is sure to be at the heart of the team's midfield.

▲ *Gerrard finds it hard to hide his emotions as England crash out of the World Cup.*

TIMELINE GLOSSARY

Team	Appearances	Goals
League		
1998–		
Liverpool	391	85
National		
1999		
England U-21	4	1
2000–		
England	89	19

Apprentice contract A training agreement between a young player and a football team, during which the footballer will receive full-time coaching and part-time education.

Caps The word used in sport to show that the player represented their national team.

Contract An agreement.

Controversial decision A decision that causes argument between people over whether it was right or wrong.

Counterattacks To fight back in response to the other team's attack.

Debut First appearance, in this case as a player in a particular team.

Ligaments Band of strong body tissue that holds two or more bones together.

Midfielder A player who plays mostly in the mid-section of the football pitch.

Penalty shootout In the event of a draw, players from each team take it in turns to score goals from the penalty spot.

Quarter-finals Eight teams compete in the quarter-finals in order to win a place in the semi-finals.

INDEX